C000263118

M I N D   T H E   G A P

Connecting faith with work

Richard Higginson

Contents

About this workbook

This is a workbook about how to relate Christian faith to the world of work. It can be used by home groups, Lent groups, or Christian fellowships in the workplace. It is divided into five chapters, the first chapter explaining why this is a crucial though neglected subject, and the next four looking at work from a series of key biblical perspectives. It is designed to be used by a group over five successive weeks. However, each chapter contains enough material for a much longer course if the group prefers: a ten-week course would enable the group to engage with the topic in greater depth.

Here are some suggestions about using this workbook. The group leader will need to read all the text in advance. The whole group may wish to as well; alternatively they can read through and discuss it together. (Group leaders may photocopy relevant sections for distribution at appropriate moments.) Each chapter contains three different activities as a 'group focus', which usually correspond to different sections of the chapter. These can either be tackled after the relevant sections, or taken together after reading through the whole chapter. Please use the material in whichever way you find most helpful.

Two things are essential for each group member. First, they must have a Bible, since they will be studying specific Bible passages at some point every week. The version I have used most of the time is the *New International Version*, with occasional use of the *Revised Standard Version*. Second, they must be willing to reflect honestly on their own experience of work.

I hope that you enjoy this workbook, and I will be very pleased to receive any feedback about it. You will find my address on the list of resources at the back.

Richard Higginson

Introduction

Work matters

'What's your name and where d'you come from?' Those questions, immortalized by Cilla Black on the TV programme *Blind Date*, are what we usually ask when we meet someone for the first time. The next question is often 'What do you do?' Let's think about the significance of that question.

For most of us, our personal identity is closely related to our work. What we do influences how we view ourselves and how others view us. So our self-worth tends to plummet when we find ourselves out of work. The fact is that *work matters*. It takes up a lot of time and energy, and it has major effects on our well-being. Given that situation, it is surprising how little interest many local churches take in the work that members of their congregation do. Often clergy are less interested in what members do during the day than in their evening and weekend church activities. The world of work is largely missing from churches' liturgy, corporate prayer and preaching.

And when it is included, it is often focused very narrowly on the 'caring professions', education, or political leadership. Every now and again the church prays for those who are at the

'In the thirty years of my professional career, my church has never once suggested that there be any type of accounting of my on-the-job ministry to others. My church has never once offered to improve those skills which could make me a better minister, nor has it ever asked if I needed any kind of support in what I am doing. There has never once been an enquiry into the types of ethical decision I must face, or whether I seek to communicate the faith to my co-workers. I have never been in a congregation where there was any type of public affirmation of the ministry in my career. In short, I must conclude that my church does not have the least interest in whether, or how, I minister in my daily life.'

A Christian sales manager

forefront of crisis situations or have the task of maintaining law and order. It hardly prays at all for those involved in any type of commercial activity. Indeed, people often find

CHAPTER 1

the idea of praying for an accountant or a sales executive laughable.

The clergy are not solely to blame. Often there is an unconscious conspiracy between members of the congregation and their leaders, to keep the messy business of work off the church's agenda. Some people come to church to escape from work; they do not want to be reminded of it, let alone challenged about it. They come for a spiritual recharge for their personal 'inner' relationship with God.

Other Christians, however, feel deeply dissatisfied when churches mark work off as a 'no-go' area. They see the work they do during the week as a form of ministry, and long for the church to take an interest in it and to nurture them for it.

Other Christians, however, feel deeply dissatisfied when churches mark work off as a 'no-go' area.

Salt and light

You may be asking why Christians should be so concerned with the world of work. If work is so important, why doesn't the Bible have more to say about it? Isn't work simply a necessary evil, a means of making ends meet so that one is then able to pursue the really fulfilling things (such as watching football matches or running youth clubs) which go on outside working hours?

Some Christians regard work as an opportunity to witness to their faith, but in a rather limited way. They invite their colleagues to occasional evangelistic events. They try to keep their standards of personal behaviour beyond reproach, a duty which often gets translated into not swearing and not stealing the paper clips! But is there more to living out our faith at work than this?

The view of this book is that all the major Christian doctrines are relevant to the world of work. What is more, we have a responsibility to think through their implications. Doing so can be exciting, even life-transforming!

Discipleship includes work

When Jesus said that his disciples were to be *salt* and *light* (Matthew 5:13-16), he was including every area of life: he says salt *of the earth* and light *of the world*. For us, in our setting, this must include the place where we spend much of our time –

> **Four key Christian doctrines you can't keep out of the workplace**
> ♦ The doctrine of *creation* tells us about the place work has in God's purposes for human beings
> ♦ The doctrine of *the fall* tells us how sin has spoilt the way work is organized and conducted
> ♦ The doctrine of *redemption* tells us how, through Christ's death on the cross, work can be changed for the better
> ♦ The doctrine of *our future hope* tells us how God is working to change things, and the ways in which we can co-operate with him

our work. Think about the various functions of salt and light:

● Salt *stings* and light *warns*: we have a responsibility to resist evil influences and be alert to moral danger in the workplace.
● Salt *flavours* and light *guides*: we have a responsibility to encourage what is good and to show how God's ways are effective and beneficial.
● Salt *preserves* and light *shines*: we have a responsibility to be true to our nature – open about our faith and applying it to everything.

Notice that Jesus doesn't give us the option of choosing when and where to be salt and light. He gives a very stern verdict on salt that has become contaminated and ineffective, or on

light which is perversely hidden away: they are good for nothing!

Work with a difference

In Romans 12:1-2, Paul applies his long explanation of Christian doctrine: 'Present your bodies as a living sacrifice, holy and acceptable to God, which is your spiritual worship.' The vision is that everything Christians do should be offered to God in his service. If we cannot include our work in that, we are not being true to God.

Paul continues: 'Do not be conformed to this world but be transformed by the renewal of your mind...' Christians in the workplace should not go along unthinkingly with the world's way of doing things. Our minds have been and are being renewed, so we may 'prove what is the will of God, what is good and acceptable and perfect'. 'Prove' in this context has the meaning of discern, identify or find out. Christians at work should be in the business of searching out God's will for any particular situation.

We all have a calling

Christians often speak of having a vocation or *calling* to the particular work that they do. The direct biblical support for this is slight, though Paul in 1 Corinthians 7:20 uses the word 'calling' about the economic status (e.g. slave or freedman) in which people find themselves. But it is consistent with the idea of God taking a personal interest in our lives and of his giving us particular *gifts* to use in his service. The skills with which God has equipped men and women include a fine eye for financial detail, agility with one's hands, resolving conflict between quarrelsome children, and much more besides! Our talents can go a long way towards making the world, not just the church, a better place.

The Protestant Reformer Martin Luther was very keen on the idea of calling. He emphasized the great variety of occupations in which it was possible to work hard and serve God. They were certainly not limited to the 'religious' occupations of priest, monk or nun. Luther insisted that the mother feeding her baby, the maid brushing the floor, or the magistrate passing sentence, were doing something of real value if they performed these tasks in response to God's command and for his glory.

The worker's prayer
Teach me, my God and King
In all things thee to see
And what I do in anything
To do it as for thee.

All may of thee partake
Nothing can be so mean
Which with this tincture *for thy sake*
Will not grow bright and clean.

George Herbert

The changing pattern of work

By 'work' most people mean 'paid employment'. But we should include lots of other activity (around the house or in the community) which is unpaid as well. Anything which contributes to human well-being can be 'work'.

Patterns of work have changed over time. A revolution happened 200 years ago. Work, which in an agricultural economy had been largely home-based, became quite separated from the home in an industrial economy when men, women and even children were lured out of the home into the new factories and mines. You went out to work at a single job, instead of a variety of tasks, and left the work behind when you came home.

For many people, that sharp separation still exists, but it is not nearly as widespread a pattern as it was. The number of people who are self-employed, and working from home as a base, is growing. The revolution in telecommunications (computers, faxes, electronic mail, etc) means that work can often be done away from the central base.

As work patterns become more flexible, so the degree of choice increases about how much you work and when you work. Charles Handy talks about acquiring a work *portfolio*. This may include a mixture of paid (part-time or contract) work, unpaid or 'gift' work (perhaps for a voluntary organization in the local community) and offering services to people in exchange for what they can do for you on a 'quid pro quo' basis.

What is work?

In *Issues Facing Christians Today* (Marshalls, 1984), John Stott describes work as 'the expenditure of energy (manual or mental or both) in the service of others, which brings fulfilment to the worker, benefit to the community and glory to God'. This is an excellent description of what work should be like, but it is probably too idealized a description to match most people's experience.

Charles Handy, perhaps Britain's leading business 'guru', defines work simply as 'useful activity'. I like that, but I think we may need to add a phrase like 'activity undertaken with a sense of obligation'. This contrasts with the sense of freedom we associate with leisure. Certainly, there may be an element of choice about the work activity we undertake, but once we have made our choice we feel obliged to those we are serving to continue that activity as long as a contract or agreement is understood to be operating. The student or housewife can feel this sense of obligation just as much as the person in paid employment.

CHAPTER 1

The number of hours which people are spending in paid employment is also changing. A generation ago, a typical pattern was to work 47 hours a week, 47 (or more) weeks of the year, for 47 years of your life (18 to 65) – which totals over 100,000 hours. Today, the total figure is likely to be nearer 50,000 hours, but they are not reducing to the neat formula 37 x 37 x 37. For full-time workers, the reduction is largely in the number of years worked; for part-time workers, in the number of hours; for temporary workers, in the number of weeks.

What the changes mean

Derek, a sixty-year-old former executive with a multinational oil company, was made redundant five years ago. He has a good pension, and now works part-time as a business consultant. He enjoys the flexibility of his present situation; it gives him more time to devote to church activities and playing golf.

Maureen is a fifty-year-old teacher in a primary school. She loves her work with children, but is finding the increasing amount of bureaucracy in education and the challenge of responding to an ever-changing National Curriculum very demanding. She feels the teaching profession is constantly under a critical spotlight. Her sense of fulfilment is declining.

Jim is a twenty-year-old unemployed shipworker. The yard where he was working closed down a year ago, and there is little prospect of further employment in the industry. He left school at sixteen with few qualifications, and is struggling to come to terms with the dwindling numbers of jobs available for semi-skilled manufacturing workers. He feels bored, frustrated and worthless.

Ros, a thirty-year-old single parent, has two small children. She is a registered child-minder for other parents, particularly dual-career couples. She is happy to provide a home-based service in this way, but resents the low wages paid to her by people who, she thinks, could afford to be far more generous.

Peter, a forty-year-old personnel manager for a leading high street bank, recently helped implement a new wave of redundancies cutting jobs to more 'efficient' levels. Morale in the bank is now very low, and people like himself who remain are having to work harder than ever to compensate for colleagues who have left. His job title has just been changed to 'Director of Human Resources'. He feels uncomfortable treating people like machines.

Andrew is aged fifty-five and took early retirement from the local authority for which he had worked all his life. His pension is sufficient to keep him and his wife modestly, and together they now divide their time between counselling for Relate, running the village hall, and looking after their young grandchildren when their daughter is overseas for her job.

Aim

*To gain a wider understanding
of the nature and purpose of work.*

1. Bible base

a Look up Matthew 5:13-16. What does it mean in practical terms to be salt and light in relation to, say, company policies, personnel management, and corner-cutting at office or shop-floor level?

b Look up Romans 12:1-3. What practical ways could you suggest to enable your fellow church members to view their work as a form of worship? What attitudes which are based more on the world's view do we need to change?

c Look up Colossians 3:22 – 4:1. In a competitive and cost-conscious world, what practical effect might Paul's teaching here have on the way we do our work? (If anyone says Paul is impractical, talk about the ways ideals could be worked towards!)

2. Change at the sharp end

Discuss the following questions in your group:

● What changing work patterns are you aware of, and how have they affected you personally?

● What has been positive and what has been negative about these changes?

● To what extent do you feel secure about your work situation?

It will be important to give each group member time to think about and voice their response to these questions. Be sensitive to their feelings. Not everyone will feel able to share very deeply at first.

GROUP FOCUS

3. Workers in the church

Get the group to brainstorm on how often they recall people in the following occupations being prayed for in church services (change the list to take account of your church or area):

	Quite often	Occasionally	Never
Ambulance workers			
Artists			
Bank managers			
Broadcasters			
Builders			
Company directors			
Engineers			
Farmers			
Lawyers			
Lorry drivers			
Nurses			
Police			
Politicians			
Retailers			
Secretaries			
Social workers			
Soldiers			
Teachers			
Unemployed people			
Union leaders			

- Discuss in the group to what extent the variety of work should be recognized in our corporate praying.

- Who decides what gets prayed for, and how could that person be better informed?

- Think of specific matters to pray for relating to your work – and share them together.

Creation

You may have seen a car sticker which says 'Work is the curse of the drinking classes'. Others are variations on the theme of 'Work is for people who can't sail'. Work, in other words, is something we would prefer to do as little of as possible. The Bible sees it quite differently. Work is one of the things we were made for.

WORK IS FOR PEOPLE WHO CAN'T SAIL

Caution: God at work!

God's acts of creation are described as work: 'By the seventh day God had finished the work he had been doing; so on the seventh day he rested from all his work' (Genesis 2:2). The previous chapter of Genesis has described in detail the careful way in which God made an orderly universe.

But God's work was not finished at creation – he is not like an absentee company chairman who has now gone off to the Bahamas on holiday! He continues to sustain the world in its ongoing existence, and he is also working to repair and restore it (more of this in chapter 4). In the middle of a sharp controversy with his Jewish opponents over healing on the sabbath, Jesus makes a very interesting comment: 'My Father is always at his work to this very day,

and I, too, am working' (John 5:17). Isaiah links God's original work of creation with his ongoing work of giving 'breath to its people' (Isaiah 42:5), and Paul refers to Jesus, the agent of creation, as the one who goes on holding everything together (Colossians 1:16,17).

His work is not just making, nor just maintaining the physical world, however; his creativity continues in the building of his church – a very different but equally vital task. For example, the growth of the Philippian church is God's 'good work' which he will complete (Philippians 1:6). But neither his activity in the physical order nor that in the social and spiritual order allows us to have a perpetual holiday; we are called to share his ongoing work.

CHAPTER 2

Made to work

In Genesis 1, human beings are told to 'subdue the earth' and 'rule over' living creatures. It hints at a major struggle with the elements, which we are given permission to master. In Genesis 2, Adam is put in the garden 'to till it and keep it'. He is given the delightful task of naming the animals. Here the relationship with nature is one of friendly companionship, and he is even given a friendly companion Eve, to help him discharge the responsibility better!

Psalm 8 echoes Genesis 1 in that it says God has made man *ruler* of creation: 'You made him ruler over the works of your hands; you put everything under his feet: all flocks and herds, and the beasts of the field' (8:6-7). It could give us dangerously swollen heads, were it not for the fact that the writer also emphasizes our *smallness* compared with the vastness of the universe. A proper humility before God should lead us to manage his world in a careful and compassionate way, not a wilful and destructive one. We are accountable to him for what we do with it: our position is that of *stewards*, not absolute rulers. Psalm 24:1 reminds us that 'the earth is the Lord's, and everything in it'. The earth should therefore be treated with respect. Here are the foundations for a 'green' theology which highlights our duty to care for the environment and to nurture, not exploit, its resources.

Again the Bible writers extend the concept of stewardship further. We are 'God's fellow-workers' in the whole of life, including the *work* of building and extending the church (1 Corinthians 3:9). In Christian theology, unlike contemporary thinking, 'work' covers much more than our paid job.

'Work is the normal, natural and healthy routine of human living; it is as obvious and regular an activity as that the sun should rise or that lions should hunt' (see Psalm 104:19-23).

Alan Richardson, A Theological Wordbook of the Bible, SCM, 1962

A chip off God's block

Genesis 1:27 says: 'So God created man in his own image, in the image of God he created him; male and female he created them.' That is a very striking statement. An image is a carved likeness. This creates a problem, because we have physical bodies but we know that God does not.

Being made in God's image includes at least:
♦ being *rational* – like God, who must have formidable intelligence, we can exercise our reason

Creative tension

Although work is necessary – and therefore may sometimes be boring or a drudge even for the most 'creative' of tasks – it is intended to exercise and extend our God-given talents and abilities. Anyone's work can in that sense be 'creative'. The qualities of God's image, such as reason, moral decision-making and relationships, feature prominently in the workplace. Working usually involves disciplined thought, it certainly throws up moral dilemmas, and it generally requires skills in relating to various types and ages of people. At its best, work offers enormous scope for allowing us to realize our potential as human beings made in God's image, resembling him and representing him on earth.

A fascinating snapshot of ordinary people working as God intended them to is found in Exodus 35:30 – 36:1. Bezalel and Oholiab are two of the unsung heroes of the Old Testament. Bezalel was a skilled carpenter, metalsmith and engraver. He led the work on the tabernacle and its precious cargo, the ark of the covenant. Oholiab was his assistant, specializing in design, weaving and embroidery. Notice three key points from this passage:

● **Bezalel and Oholiab are *filled with the Spirit of God***. This phrase is used sparingly in the Old Testament, usually reserved for individuals in the roles of prophet, priest or king. Here it is used for the skills of the

♦ being *moral* – like God, we can distinguish between right and wrong, and are responsible for our actions

♦ being *spiritual* – like God, we have a capacity for eternal life, and we are aware of a spiritual dimension to life

♦ being *relational* – like God, who relates within himself in the different persons of the Trinity, we can relate personally to God and others

♦ being *creative* – like God, whose immense creativity is seen in his creation of the world, human beings can beget and make things

♦ being *reflective* – like God, we are aware of ourselves as unique and distinct persons, who can reflect creatively and imaginatively on our lives, and make art

♦ *exercising authority* – in humanity's case an authority delegated by God over the rest of creation.

The Bible never defines the image of God as a single one of these qualities. We need an understanding of the divine image which takes in the entirety of the human person, not a narrow, one-dimensional view. Each aspect can – and should – relate to our work in its broad and narrow senses.

CHAPTER 2

craftsman. God's Spirit encompasses the fashioning of material things – hardly surprising, since that same Spirit was involved in the same activity in Genesis 1.

● **Bezalel and Oholiab are *equipped by God for their work*.** The qualities mentioned include ability, intelligence, knowledge, craftsmanship, skills in specific materials, and – not least – inspiration to teach. The gift of

teaching needs, of course, to be practised not just in schools and colleges but in all types of work.

● **Bezalel and Oholiab e*xercised creativity*.** This is implicit in the emphasis on design and the variety of colours, materials and forms which they used. The Spirit of God released their imaginations to create something new, striking and memorable. In our work we need to be open to that same inspiration.

Adding value

How may we begin to apply these biblical emphases to the world of work today?

On one hand, we can make some very positive comments. A crucial part of managing God's creation is the wise use of the world's resources.

God has so made the world that most of its resources (e.g. oil, cotton, sugar) require some process of extraction, conversion and refinement before they can be of benefit. Many of these resources remained unused until the technological developments of the eighteenth and nineteenth centuries made their development possible.

The essence of manufacturing industry is *adding value to original resource*. That is the only way many of God's gifts can be of benefit to us. The more sophisticated the industry,

of course, the more processed is the nature of the primary material, such as the micro-chip in the construction of computers. Many of the heavy manufacturing industries have now declined, and we have moved towards a greater emphasis on ancillary or service industries. But there are still three good reasons for

> 'The earth, by reason of its fruitfulness and its capacity to satisfy human needs, is God's first gift for the sustenance of human life. But the earth does not yield its fruits without a particular human response to God's gift, that is to say, without work.'
>
> *Pope John Paul II*, Centesimus Annus

giving jobs which *make things* a central place in our understanding of work:

● Developing material resources in ever more efficient and ingenious ways will never stop. God has given human beings an inventive streak.
● The service industries need something to service. Manufacturing industry still makes up a very significant part of their client base.
● A successful product has considerable potential for creating wealth. And this is good news, not just for the firm's employees (to keep them in a job) but also for society because a thriving business sector raises more taxation and makes possible a more generous provision of public services. Doctors, teachers, social workers and all the people we more readily pray for in church do many valuable things, but it would be extremely difficult to afford them without the wealth creation provided by industry.

On the other hand, there is a dark side to industry which cannot be ignored. We might be better off without some of the material goods which are made. The record of many is highly ambiguous, e.g. the motor car is a quick and convenient form of transport, but it regularly kills and maims people and animals, and pollutes the atmosphere. Global warming, the consequence of industrial development, threatens the delicate balance of the world's atmosphere. So we must not be glib

about using the phrase *wealth creation.* Companies which make trash products or seriously damage the environment are not creating wealth or being good stewards in any lasting sense. They are destroying value more than adding it.

'O Lord our God, your creation holds within it such abundant promise for all your people. You have entrusted us with the stewardship of the earth, and opened before us a vision of what can be achieved. You have given us a capacity to meet the needs of those who lack good things, to experience satisfaction through our daily work, and to use the resources you have showered upon us responsibly. Help us to realize these hopes and fulfil this trust. For Christ's sake, Amen.'

CHAPTER 2

What makes for happy work?

Pleasant conditions Congenial surroundings with satisfactory heating and lighting do make a difference.

Making use of talents We do not always get a good match between our work and our particular talents, but when we do, work feels better.

Control over the work Sometimes we feel how, when and where we do our work is totally controlled by others. If we are able to organize these things for ourselves, it's much more satisfying.

Exercising responsibility Responsibility can be a burden but it can also be a privilege and challenge. We are aware that a lot depends on the quality of our work, and this often brings the best out of others.

Designing or making something new Novelty usually spells excitement. Of course, there is risk involved, but at least work's not dull when innovation is in the air.

Stimulation Work is stimulating when it stretches us, by having fascinating people around us, the advent of new technology, or simply a particular challenge.

Team work When team members enjoy each other's company, co-operate well, encourage each other, play to their strengths and minimize

their weaknesses, work can be extremely satisfying.

Achievement This is often the outcome of effective teamwork. Targets are reached by deadlines we did not think possible without sacrificing quality.

Seeing the purpose One of the problems with the way work has traditionally been fragmented (the classic example being the assembly line) is that workers only see their bit of the product, not the final product itself. Management consultant Christian Schumacher feels that work should be organized around key moments of *transformation* to which every worker contributes.

Benefitting others There are different ways of expressing this. You might talk in terms of satisfying the client or customer, or you may use the language of serving and helping people. Either way, the focus is on the benefits which accrue to others.

Appreciation Those little words 'Thank you' and 'Well done' can make an enormous difference. We like to know that our contribution has been noticed.

Earning money Let's not be so spiritually minded that we pretend this is of no importance! It is often (not always) a sign of work well done and a measure of satisfaction.

Aim

To discover some positive
approaches to work in the world.

1. Bible base

Give group members one or more of these verses each to look up, think
about, and then to tell the others: 'What does this verse say about the
nature and purpose of work in God's world?'

- Genesis 1:28
- Genesis 2:15
- Exodus 20:9-11
- Psalm 8:3-9
- Psalm 104:19-23
- Psalm 127:1,2
- Ecclesiastes 2:24,25
- Isaiah 45:18
- Acts 20:33-35
- 1 Corinthians 3:7-10
- Ephesians 4:28
- 2 Thessalonians 3:6-13

2. Think creatively

How might we help each other to see our paid work more creatively?
Discuss with group members how they see their tasks as contributing to
the organization, the client, and their colleagues. Use this discussion to
focus on the biblical concept that work, while it can be personally
fulfilling, is also for others' benefit.

GROUP FOCUS

3. Happy workers?

Think about the positive aspects of work in your group. When you *have* found work (paid or unpaid) to be satisfying, and when you have (if only vaguely and sub-consciously) had a sense of being a co-creator with God, why was this so? What were the crucial factors about the work you were doing?

The table below lists factors which can play an important part in making work a creative and satisfying experience. If you have experienced work of this sort, tick the box marked 'Yes?', and briefly describe the work episode in the box next to it. Some boxes are left empty for you to add other factors that you feel are significant.

Positive factor	Yes?	Where and when?
The work was done in pleasant conditions		
I felt I was making use of my particular talents		
I had control over the work I was doing		
I was exercising considerable responsibility		
The work involved designing or making something new		
The work was very stimulating		
I was part of a team which worked well together		
A great deal was achieved in a short time		
I could see the end results of the work		
The work brought benefits to other people		
The work I did was appreciated by colleagues		
The work brought in plenty of money		
?		
?		
?		

Now compare your experiences in the group.

Fall

The smell of failure

The world today is far from what God intended. It is like a train that has gone off the rails. Christians explain this in terms of the world being *fallen*. It expresses the fact that human beings have fallen from the high position that God gave them. They deviate from God's purposes for them and his world in many ways. This has serious consequences. In work, as in other places, there is the smell of failure – or what the Bible calls 'sin'.

Here are seven ways in which the fallen state of our world is seen in the workplace:

Frustration Work can often be extremely frustrating. We work hard over something and achieve nothing. The house that a parent spends all day tidying up is systematically untidied by the small child who trails round after him or her. The key report which the secretary had devotedly typed up is lost for ever when the computer crashes. The client with the drugs problem seems to be responding to treatment, and then undoes all the progress in an evening's wild partying.

The Bible includes some vivid pictures of frustration at work. Genesis 3:17-19 speaks of sweat and toil, thorns and thistles. The writer of Ecclesiastes felt his work to be a 'chasing after the wind...What does a man get for all the toil and anxious striving with which he labours under the sun? All his days his work is pain and grief; even at night his mind

The house that a parent spends all day tidying up is systematically untidied by the small child who trails round after him or her.

19

CHAPTER 3

does not rest' (2:17,22-23). Peter and his fellow-disciples had the exasperating experience of fishing all night – which *was* the best time to fish – and catching nothing (John 21:1-3).

Alienation Work is repeatedly bedevilled by poor relationships. People treat each other without respect. They are quick to blame each other when things go wrong. 'Us' and 'them' conflicts develop between management and unions, teachers and children, marketing and research departments. People also feel that their work (especially menial work) alienates them from true fulfilment.

The Bible traces this alienation back to human beings' original disobedience. Our relationship to God was damaged, and so was our relationship with each other. Genesis 3 emphasizes the damaging consequences for the relationship between the sexes. Woman now encounters man's way of relating to her in the form of 'rule' (3:16). In the workplace, this has often resulted in discrimination – low pay, lack of promotion, and sexual harassment. Genesis 4 describes how alienation spreads through jealousy, leading to violence.

Isolation Most people work alongside others. But isolation takes many forms. In chapter one we noted the sharp separation between work and home which took place with industrialization. For many people this is still true: their spouse or children have never been inside the office or factory where they work. A split life can create a split personality, and we struggle to integrate the two halves of our existence. Now, with the growing popularity of home-working, there is an opposite problem. You may see more of the family, but you miss the social interaction with other people. Communicating by e-mail is an inadequate substitute.

Christians may also feel isolated in the workplace *as Christians* . They may feel out of sympathy with the prevailing ethos – the jokes, the assumptions, the dishonest expense-claims. They may long for some kindred spirits who share their priorities and concerns. A crowd is a lonely place when you are supporting a different team, or even when you have mixed loyalties.

Laceration A lacerated world is one that is torn and wounded. It may bring to mind the huge gashes in the countryside caused by mining or construction, or the hole in the ozone layer caused by insensitive use of CFCs. But it also expresses the deep, ugly and untidy divisions which exist between people and organizations. The world of work is *scarred*. To survive, you have to operate according to the law of the jungle: a case of looking after yourself and getting your retaliation in first.

Competition is a fact of life, and it can be a spur to excellence and provide a better deal for the customer. But it also brings in its wake dubious practices like poaching employees, derogatory advertising, and paying bribes to win contracts. In recent years, schools and hospitals which used to understand their relationship with other schools and hospitals to be co-operative and complementary have increasingly been set up to compete with each other.

Unclear Vocation In chapter one we noted the concept of each person having a calling to their work. But it is not always easy to know what this is. Our gifts may point us in a bewildering variety of directions. Our parents or friends may think we're suited for one line of work but we don't agree. We may have tried several different things but none have really worked out. We're not sure how God wants to use us.

Alternatively, we may have a very clear sense of what we want or ought to be doing. The problem is that circumstances are preventing us from carrying it out. The firm where we had a satisfying job has gone bankrupt. Supply is exceeding demand for our skills, so the odds are stacked against us when we apply for jobs. The needs of family are keeping us at home, with the result that our talents are lying dormant. There is often a mismatch between our skills and what work is available.

Regimentation When work is regimented, people are subjected to

excessive control. What they do and how they do it is governed by strict rules and regulations. Of course, most work needs an element of this – who wants to travel with an airline that does not carry out rigorous safety checks on its engine mountings? But too much control is oppressive to the human spirit. It discourages initiative and stifles people's natural creativity.

Regimentation is often associated with an assembly line which restricts each individual to performing one task. In *The Wealth of Nations*, published in 1776, economist Adam Smith described with approval a method of making pins, 'divided into about eighteen distinct operations, which, in some manufactories, are all performed by distinct hands'. In his book *To Live and Work*, Christian Schumacher calls this sort of regimented, soul-destroying work 'deformed'. The fact that people came to be known as *hands* (suggesting that was the only part of their body which was really valued) is itself significant. Today, they are known as human resources, which is not much better – the stress is still on what they are useful for, not on who they are.

Exploitation In many working situations, those who own or manage the enterprise have considerable power over those employed lower down the line. They may pay them a pittance, subject them to dangerous working conditions, force them to work long hours, or sack them

CHAPTER 3

without cause. In some countries there is legal protection against such practices, but in many it is very weak. The potential for exploitation at work is immense. In the West, the pressure may be more subtle – work extra hours or we all go under.

In the Bible the Egyptian taskmasters made the Israelites' 'lives bitter with hard labour in brick and mortar and with all kinds of work in the fields' (Exodus 1:13-14). King Solomon employed forced labour in building the temple and palace, work which must have lacked compensating features, because it contributed to a rebellion under his son Rehoboam (1 Kings 5-12). In Revelation 18, a vivid picture of the city of Rome under judgment, the cargo whose loss the merchants mourn includes 'slaves, that is human souls'. There is an implicit criticism here of the slave trade. Human beings should not be bought and sold as chattels.

F rustration
A lienation
I solation
L aceration
U nclear Vocation
R egimentation
E xploitation

Lord, we're sorry for the bad things which spoil the world of work. Forgive us when we're blind to them; forgive us when we contribute to them. Give us a longing for wholesome work, cleansed of all these failings.
For Jesus' sake, Amen.

How to make hard decisions

Christian ideals have to be worked out in less than ideal situations. Often it's not clear what we should do or even what we can hope to do. Here are some stepping stones to help you get from facing a problem to taking appropriate action.

1. Consider the relevant facts.
Try to get as full a picture of the work situation as possible, taking into account the relevant facts. This may well include what the position of the law is on the issue concerned.

2. Identify the vital principles.
They may be qualities you can sum up in a single word, like honesty, integrity, loyalty, compassion or forgiveness. They may be principles that are expressed in a well-established phrase like the sanctity of life or the reduction of suffering.

3. Accept that there may be no ideal solution.
Whatever you do, there are undesirable consequences. But we do not have to express a dilemma in negative terms. Looked at from one perspective, we are choosing the lesser evil; looked at from another, it is about discerning the greater good.

4. Consult the important sources of guidance. Sometimes valuable guidance may be available from a secular source, e.g. a company or professional code, or an experienced colleague of good character and reliable judgment. But often we will want to consult specifically Christian sources of guidance, for example:

● the Bible – there may be specific passages which relate to the issue
● Christian doctrine – to put the problem within the context of the major truths of our faith
● the story of the Church – we may find help in the example of what other Christian individuals or groups have done in similar situations.

5. Analyze the alternatives. There are usually more than two possible courses of action. When confronted by a dilemma, we need to think creatively and imaginatively. The best solution may not be obvious at first sight.

6. Recognize that your position makes a difference. Dilemmas look different depending on where you find yourself in your organization. At the top, you may have more freedom in setting moral direction. Further down, you are expected to obey orders, and the security of your job or your promotion prospects may be in jeopardy if you object. You have to make finely balanced judgments about how much a particular issue *matters*.

7. Evaluate an order of priorities. This is the difficult bit! You may be able to find a neat solution which keeps the different principles in balance, but the chances are that you will have to shift the balance in a particular direction, in other words *weigh* the various principles. One may have to be put ahead of another.

8. Take the decision prayerfully before God. Praying can have the great effect of clarifying the mind. Even if it doesn't, it is vital to commit the situation into God's hands. You may be troubled by the feeling that whatever you decide, it bears the mark of sin. But as Martin Luther said, 'Believe even more boldly and rejoice in Christ!' Have the courage to make the decision and go forward, secure in the promise of God's love and forgiveness.

'Unemployment is not a problem of statistics but of people. In the Third World, where no wage-related unemployment benefit is available, it is often a question of actual survival, but in the West the suffering is more psychological than physical. It is a poignant personal and social tragedy.'

John Stott, Issues Facing Christians Today, Marshalls, 1984, p 164

GROUP FOCUS

Aim

To understand why work is often frustrating,
and to think practically about ways of supporting those in
difficult work situations.

1. Bible base

What can you discover from these passages about the causes and effects of
drudgery and imperfection in work? How do they relate to the experience
of group members?

- Genesis 3:16-19
- Ecclesiastes 2:11,17-23
- Isaiah 44:6-20
- James 4:13 – 5:6

Reflect together, too, on the seven marks of fallenness described earlier.
What is your experience of them and their causes?

2. Help the unemployed

One of the worst aspects of fallenness as it affects us today is
unemployment. How might the church help people who are unemployed?
Be practical and visionary; perhaps after prayer you could *do* something,
however small, within your own church or area.

3. Face the dilemmas!

We have to live in the world as we know it. We work in the midst of
turmoil, trying to do the best we can. Yet we often feel that our power to
change things is very limited, that we act with at least one hand tied. We
operate under the constraints of a fallen world.

The way in which this hits us most strongly is when we are faced by moral
dilemmas in the workplace which seem to involve us in sin or evil
whichever route we choose. Consider the following scenarios, working
through the steps outlined on pages 22-23 to make your decisions.
Alternatively, look at real situations group members face.

NEIL is the managing director of a medium-sized engineering firm. Denis,
who is thirty-seven, has been its marketing manager for the last six years.
He was once full of enthusiasm, good ideas and had an excellent track
record and network of contacts. Recently, however, he has become casual,
appears lazy and communicates poorly with his deputy. He has also
developed a drink problem – his speech after lunch is often slurred and he

has behaved embarrassingly at evening meetings. Six months ago Neil challenged Denis about his performance and his drinking. He resolved to improve and for a time did so, but during the last month has failed to meet work targets and his alcohol consumption has again risen. What should Neil do? And why?

CLARE is a doctor in general practice who is concerned about the extent and health risks of under-age sex among young teenagers. One evening, fifteen-year-old Jessica comes to her surgery and with considerable embarrassment asks to go on the pill. She has a sixteen-year-old boyfriend whom she has known for three years, and with whom she says she has had unprotected sex a couple of times. He refuses to use a condom, and she had a scare recently when her period was late. Clare suggests that Jessica should talk about contraception with her parents, but Jessica claims they would be angry and it would not be any use. Legally, Clare is allowed to prescribe the pill to someone under sixteen if she feels that there is a need for contraception to avoid pregnancy, but understandably she does not wish to. What should Clare do? And what factors might influence her decision as a professional and as a Christian?

TOM is a coach driver on long-distance routes. His firm is experiencing aggressive competition, during a recession, from an unscrupulous rival. This is forcing Tom's firm to cut costs wherever possible. Tom has recently been told by his boss that he must be prepared to fit in an extra fifty-mile journey each day, even though this will take him beyond the number of hours he is allowed to drive by law. The firm's view is that if it abides strictly by the law it will have to employ more drivers than it can afford. 'The company's survival is at stake' is what his boss tells Tom when he objects. Tom remains unhappy about breaking the law, although he thinks an extra fifty miles is within his capacity to manage safely. The extra hours bring in useful overtime pay, but they are obviously encroaching on his time with his family at a time when his children are very demanding. What should Tom do? And why?

JANE is a production manager. Her company has a large, prestigious contract. But her materials supplier has gone bust, and the only replacement available is of inferior quality. The chief engineer is off with a broken leg, and a flash flood has damaged some of the firm's machinery. The client is getting impatient, threatening financial sanctions (before lunch) and taking away his custom altogether (at 4.55 p.m.). The firm is already stretched, but if it loses this order it could lose its place in the market or even go out of business altogether. What should Jane do? And why?

CHAPTER 4

Reconciliation

Finding Christ at work

For many Christians, relating their faith to their work does not get beyond what we have considered so far. If you are in an unsatisfying job, or you are conscious of low standards of behaviour in your workplace, the *fall* is likely to be uppermost in your mind. If you are fortunate enough to have a stimulating job in which you can develop your gifts, you may be more influenced by the doctrine of *creation*. In fact, what most of us experience, most of the time, is a mixture of the two: creation-with-fall. In other words, God's gracious provision of work, grievously flawed. But these key Old Testament ideas are not enough. We need to consider what makes for a distinctively Christian view of work.

When Christ is making a difference to how we think about the workplace and what we do in it, this gives us confidence to speak about him. Our actual lives should be 'letters of recommendation' (2 Corinthians 3:1) – we might even say *advertisements*. But there comes a time for explaining what it is that motivates us. Colleagues at work have spiritual needs; we may be the only Christian they know who can pray for them, explain the gospel, and invite them to appropriate evangelistic events. Of course, we need great sensitivity in this. The Bible-basher is likely to have the effect of putting people off. The person who speaks honestly of their personal faith when the occasion is appropriate may well attract them to Christ.

At first sight the New Testament does not seem to offer many pointers to finding Christ at work. Paul's letters are mostly about church life; there is relatively little about how Christians

The Bible-basher is likely to have the effect of putting people off.

> 'We are not called to storm the gates of unbelief. We are called to move humbly, sensitively and observantly behind the Holy Spirit, and to be ready to offer a word in season when he opens up the way. Chances to turn the conversation may well come our way after a TV programme or perhaps during a discussion about a moral issue like abortion or big-business profits.'
>
> *Michael Green*, Evangelism through the Local Church, *Hodder & Stoughton 1990, p 260*

are meant to behave in their jobs. Jesus told stories about workers, but usually in order to make a point about God's relationship with us rather than to teach about work as such. Jesus' early life was spent as a carpenter (Mark 6:3) – but we know nothing in detail about this, and he never refers to it in his teaching. He even called his closest disciples *away* from their daily occupations of fishing and collecting taxes to follow him.

The New Testament does have enormous implications for the world of work, but its message is more *indirect* than direct. It needs to be teased out and thought through.

Serving one another

In Philippians 2:7-8, Paul says that Christ Jesus 'made himself nothing, taking the very nature of a servant, being made in human likeness. And being found in appearance as a man, he humbled himself...' For God to become man was a great act of humility, but the type of man he became demonstrated humility all the more. 'I am among you as one who serves,' said Jesus on the night before his death (Luke 22:27), giving his disciples a vivid example of humble service when he washed and dried their feet (John 13:1-16). The Old Testament passages which seem to have been crucial for his self-

understanding were the 'Suffering Servant' passages of Isaiah 42, 44, 49 and 53.

For Jesus, service was much more than doing things to help others. It was an act of total self-sacrifice, so difficult that even he shrank from its ultimate expression while in the Garden of Gethsemane.

In our society, servants in the traditional sense are thin on the ground – although part-time nannies and home helps are much in demand. But the concept of *service* is still alive. We associate it mostly with

CHAPTER 4

The manager gets his hands dirty clearing up a mess on the floor.

Service with a smile

◆ The supervisor goes out of her way to educate and encourage the employee struggling with new technology

◆ The librarian acts quickly to find a book that a customer was having difficulty in tracing

◆ The company repairs malfunctioning parts readily or replaces old with new

◆ The manager gets his hands dirty clearing up a mess on the floor

the caring professions such as nursing where the financial rewards are slight but the satisfaction in caring for people can be immense. But we also talk about the civil service, financial services and even the service sector. The words 'serving the customer' pass the businessman's lips often enough.

Phrases like 'making that additional effort' and 'going the extra mile' describe quality service. Often it surprises people because they expect something more routine or grudging. Some organizations even aim to *delight* the customer.

If Christians at work are taking their lead from Jesus, they should have a strong commitment to serving others. They should be sensitive to others' needs and quick to meet them. It is all too easy for the person on the other side of the desk – whether a pupil, passenger or patient – to be a source of irritation. Why

can't they behave better, or make up their mind, or stop being such a windbag? If we really take the ideal of service to heart, we hold our tongue, exercise patience and continue to seek the best interests of the customer, client or colleague.

But the Christian concept of service goes deeper than this. Many organizations talk enthusiastically about serving the customer, but the bottom line is the profit motive. Some even justify good service because it brings higher returns. Of course, profits *are* important; business cannot operate without them. But Jesus stood conventional wisdom on its head. 'Love your enemies... give, and it will be given to you... the last will be first, and the first will be last.' We should have the courage to reverse the world's view of the relationship between profit and service. Not *service as the means, to profit as the end*, but *profit as the means, to service as the end*.

Jesus ties the ends together

In Colossians 1:15-20 Paul emphasizes that Christ is not only head of the Church but Lord of the world.

● Jesus gives us GUT

Scientists have been searching for a Grand Unified Theory (GUT) which holds together the diversity of a complex and apparently random world. Jesus, the creator and sustainer, gives us a Grand Unified Theology. In verse 17, Paul claims: 'He is before all things, and in him all things hold together.' We can see Jesus as doing this both on the level of physics (upholding the constancy of the laws of nature) and on the level of metaphysics (providing life with meaning and purpose). Jesus Christ is a living person who is interested in every aspect of our lives. If all things hold together in Christ on a cosmic level, then we can be confident that he is helping us hold our bit of the world together.

● Jesus takes on the system

Paul includes under 'all things' in verse 16 'things in heaven and on earth... visible and invisible, whether thrones or powers or rulers or authorities'. Many powerful cultural forces shape our lives, such as the market economy, advertising, and our political system. Paul says that they all originate in the creative activity of Christ. However, none is free from the influence of evil. All need to be brought under the

authority of Christ. So verse 20 says that God's purpose in Christ is 'to reconcile to himself all things ... by making peace through his blood, shed on the cross'. Through Jesus' death God puts right our relationship with himself and each other. But it doesn't end there. The reconciling work of Jesus includes the world of things, powers and structures as well.

● Jesus brings peace with justice

The word *reconcile* involves the idea of making peace based on justice, in which people and structures are restored to the relationship God intends for them. It includes putting right things that are wrong. A reconciled market economy would abandon the idolatrous claims sometimes made for it, where there was as much concern about a fair distribution of wealth as there was encouragement to create it.

● Jesus helps us make a start

Clearly, not everything has yet reached the state of harmony God intends. In Romans 8:22, Paul says that 'the whole creation has been groaning as in the pains of childbirth right up to the present time'. The creation will be liberated from its bondage to decay at a future time. But we should not underestimate the difference that Christ's coming has already made. Jesus Christ sets before us the possibility of a new start – individually and organizationally. He

CHAPTER 4

has released a force for good in the world – the Holy Spirit – so that at least some of the unsatisfactory aspects of working life can be changed. And he calls those who are already reconciled to him through their personal faith to be his agents of change in the as-yet unreconciled world.

The cost of reconciliation

True reconciliation involves radical transformation of a situation, and this is rarely possible without cost. If work is to operate in the way that God desires, individuals and groups have to be prepared for self-sacrifice. Christians should not be surprised. What did it cost Jesus to reconcile the world? *It cost him his life.* How does Paul say God made peace in Jesus? *By the blood of his cross* (Colossians 1:20).

For Jesus, a servant lifestyle led to a self-sacrificial death. His disciples squabbled about who was the greatest, and tried to reserve for themselves the best seats in the kingdom of heaven (Mark 10:35-45). Jesus contrasts their attitude, typical of many, with his own approach, which the disciples should copy: 'whoever wants to become great among you must be your servant, and whoever wants to be first must be slave of all' (10:43). For himself, this meant the ultimate sacrifice. It meant going to the cross, to 'give his life as a ransom for many' (10:45). Jesus paid a price, so that human beings imprisoned in sin and selfishness might go free.
Clearly, Jesus' death was unique. But there is a basic principle here which is of wider relevance. Are we prepared to accept cost to ourselves for the sake of others? Are we willing to accept that if organizations and structures are to change significantly for the better, there is bound to be pain and suffering along the way?

This has personal applications for all of us. A firm which is struggling against tough competition might have a much better motivated staff if those at the top were prepared to forgo big salary increases and financial perks. Producers in Third World countries might get a much fairer deal if more consumers in the West were prepared to pay a little extra for products like CaféDirect and Mascao chocolate. But self-interest – individual and group self-interest – gets in the way of change.

Aim

To think creatively about ways in which we can act as reconcilers in our work, and how our work can be transformed by our understanding of Christ's life and death.

1. Bible base

Read Ephesians 2:11-22; Colossians 1:18-23; 2 Corinthians 5:14 – 6:2 (perhaps dividing into three groups). What do the passages teach about who is reconciled to whom, how the reconciliation is achieved, and what are its practical implications for daily life? Make a list of the groups' answers and then:

● discuss how we might become better agents of reconciliation
● pray together about situations where reconciliation is needed.

2. Ambassadors

Ambassadors represent their country and speak for their leader. We are ambassadors for Christ (2 Corinthians 5:20). Make a list of ways in which the church could help group members in personal witness at work. What are the opportunities? What teaching and support do you need? How might you begin to encourage that support?

3. How would you help?

Here are three stories, based on real-life situations. Discuss the problems and how a costly Christ-likeness could be demonstrated in each:

No use any more?

Martin is the founder and chairman of a high-tech company which expanded rapidly during its first five years under his dynamic leadership. Martin's skills lie in his technical expertise and capacity to enthuse staff with new ideas. He is less adept at day-to-day management, and the company has hit hard times. The board brings in a new managing director, Norman, believing his more systematic approach will complement Martin's talents. After an initial honeymoon period, relations between the two become frosty, to the point where the board decides one of them must go. Martin is aghast that it turns out to be him.

An organization which originally called for the dynamic and innovatory gifts of the entrepreneur may in time require a less flamboyant period of consolidation and a different style of leadership. But how hard it is for a founder-owner to let go! There is a real element of self-sacrifice involved.

GROUP FOCUS

How would you have helped and advised Martin:

- as the company grew rapidly
- when the need for change became obvious?

It's not my fault!

Sid is a technical service engineer. In his routine maintenance work he often receives a mouthful from customers complaining of faulty goods or a late delivery. He is often tempted to say, with a jerk of the thumb: 'It wasn't me, it was them back at the works', because others in his company are responsible for mistakes that have been made. But he has learnt to hold his tongue. He finds that it is much more constructive, because he is much more likely to reconcile the customer, if he finds the grace to say 'I'm sorry' on behalf of his organization. But his patience is wearing thin. How might he continue to be a reconciler and peacemaker?

Why can't we work together?

Liz and her marketing team work for a well-known national charity, whose aims are very similar to another leading charity. Theirs is the older organization; the other has demonstrated greater energy and attracted more financial support in recent years. There is an unhealthy rivalry between the two organizations. Market research suggests that it would make sense for the two charities to merge. Donations and resources could be used more effectively; public campaigning and media relations would be radically simplified. Liz's team decide to recommend a merger, with the other organization being allowed to take the senior role.

Corporate institutions are expected – almost by definition – to fight for their survival. But sometimes their fundamental aims can best be fulfilled by joining another organization. It's not easy.

Your task is to convince your loyal but sceptical supporters that a merger is a good idea. How do you go about it?

Future hope

So far we have looked at three stages in the biblical drama of salvation – creation, fall and redemption – and seen how they relate to the world of work. The fourth and final stage concerns *our future hope* as Christians.

New heaven, new earth

The Bible contains many passages which look ahead to events which have not yet taken place. It is not easy to know how to interpret these. Do they refer to things we can expect to happen on earth, or to a new kind of existence in heaven? To illustrate the problem, look at Isaiah 65:17-25 which suggests:

● A coming 'Golden Age' of joy, fruitfulness, contentment and harmony.
● This 'Golden Age' is pictured within the confines of earthly history and focused on Jerusalem (verse 18). People will live to a good old age (verse 20), and houses will still be built and vineyards planted.
● The vision has not yet been realized on earth. We live in a world where young people are still tragically cut short in their prime – contrast verse 20. We live in a world of annexations and hostile takeovers – contrast verse 22. We live in a world where animals still prey on each other – contrast verse 25.

Christians have different views about whether to expect a Golden Age on earth. Some feel that this is a prophecy whose time has not yet come. Others feel that the prophecy will be fulfilled in a way beyond the prophet's own understanding; he is using picture-language which points to a different quality of life after our time on earth is over. Indeed, Isaiah 65 hints at a radical difference between now and the future when it says 'I will create new heavens and a new earth' (verse 17). This phrase is picked up in Revelation 21, which clearly refers to the end time.

My own view is that the second interpretation is more likely to be correct. The world which we know is groaning; there is no indication of a Golden Age around the corner. But this should not mean that we abandon the dimension of hope, or that we pin all our longings for a better world on a heavenly hereafter. The hope which we have ought to excite us so much that it spurs us to work for the transformation of the present.

CHAPTER 5

What will we do in heaven?

The assumption that heaven is one long church service (even if it is a very good one) is not an attractive prospect for many people! The example of Jesus' resurrection body suggests that life after death will be 'the same but different'; there will be a continuity with what we have known on earth, but it will be of a vastly superior quality and in an entirely new – and perfect – context. Therefore we can assume that the best aspects of work – creativity, fulfilment, service – will have their heavenly counterparts. The Bible suggests four key themes to life there.

Worship Worship is essentially a confession of worth – God's worth, focused in the person of Jesus Christ. The New Testament contains some memorable pictures of Jesus receiving the worship he deserves, for example Philippians 2:9-11; Revelation 5:6-14. But worship is not so far removed from work as we might think. The same Hebrew word *avoda* is used to mean both: sometimes work and sometimes worship, depending on the context. Similarly, the Greek word *ergon* lies at the root of our word 'liturgy'. Our English word 'service' can of course describe work and worship.

Indeed, work which is carried out to the glory of God can be close to worship, a way of proclaiming his worth. Saint Benedict said 'To work is to pray.' Worship, well carried out, contains an element of work. There is purposeful activity involved. The worship we will offer to God in heaven will be work translated and transformed into another dimension. It will engage the energies and talents of all who know and love the Lord Jesus, whatever the type of work they do on earth.

Rest God rested on the seventh day and commanded us to do the same (Genesis 2:3; Exodus 20:8-11). Even if the sabbath does not have the same significance for Christians as it does for Jews, the principle of regular weekly rest from work remains a sound one. The workaholic is not being true to his or her created humanity.

The letter to the Hebrews takes the concept further and looks forward to a future rest for God's people: 'There remains, then, a Sabbath-rest for the people of God; for anyone who enters God's rest also rests from his own work, just as God did from his' (4:9). The theme of the saints enjoying a heavenly rest from their labours is also found in Revelation 14:13. The laboriousness of earthly work – the curse of the fall – will be over and our activity, whatever it is, will be a joy. And there will be no more committee meetings!

Judgment Paul asserts that 'we will all stand before God's judgment seat' (Romans 14:10). Peter speaks of

God cares passionately about the way we conduct our lives.

judgment beginning with the family of God (1 Peter 4:17). True, this should not alarm Christians. It would if we were relying on our own efforts, but that shouldn't be the case. There is only one way we can stand before God justified – restored to a right relationship with him – and that is through his grace: his undeserved acceptance of us through Christ's death and resurrection.

Nevertheless, God's grace is not cheap. It would be a travesty of the gospel to pretend that what we do on earth is unimportant. God cares passionately about the way we conduct our lives. In Romans 14 Paul explains the reality of judgment in terms of each of us giving account of ourselves to God (14:12). There will be something akin to a *personal audit*, when we will account for what we have done with the abilities, opportunities and resources he has put at our disposal. We will be like the servants in the parable, explaining to the master how we have invested the talents he entrusted to us (Matthew 25:14-30).

This *must* include the way we have used those talents at work. We cannot seriously expect God to enquire what we did at home, at church and in the community, and to show no interest in what we were doing during the majority of daylight hours!

In the parable, the master gave his faithful servants more responsible jobs after his return. This perhaps stresses the value of our work now and indicates a degree of continuity in heaven, which develops fully the creative gifts that are central to our personalities.

Restoration Jesus said, 'I am making everything new' (Revelation 21:5). But the picture is not of God scrapping his entire creation, like a frustrated craftsman smashing the carving or vase that has gone wrong. He is *renewing* his creation, restoring it to its original harmony and making it even more glorious than it was originally. That is the meaning of Jesus' work of reconciling all things (Colossians 1:20). In Revelation 21:24-26 the kings of the earth bring into the heavenly city 'the glory and honour of the nations'. Michael Wilcock, in his commentary on Revelation, suggests that 'all that is truly good and beautiful will reappear there, purified and enhanced in the perfect setting its Master intended for it; nothing of real value is lost'. What we do now is swept up into God's eternal purposes, and need not be wasted if we are doing it for him.

CHAPTER 5

In the meantime

The message of the kingdom of God dominated Jesus' teaching. His ministry began with his announcing 'The time has come... the kingdom of God is near' (Mark 1:15). He taught about the kingdom through his parables, and gave a visual demonstration of the kingdom through his healings. He proclaimed the mercy and justice of God, and invited people back to a restored relationship with God and with each other. The essence of the kingdom is an acknowledgment of God as king.

Jesus spoke of the kingdom both in a present and a future tense. People enter the kingdom *now* (Matthew 21:31), and it is 'in the midst of you' (Luke 17:21). But it will also come with power, some time in the future (Mark 9:1), an event which is linked to Jesus' own return in glory. The kingdom has already begun; we have seen its great and glorious dawn in the first coming of Jesus. But many still fail to accept the rule of God in their lives, and so the full arrival of the kingdom awaits his second coming. In the meantime, we are to live so that Jesus' life, death and resurrection make a difference to us and to the small corner of the world where he has placed us.

In the Lord's Prayer, we pray that God's kingdom will come, and then, 'Your will be done, on earth as it is in heaven'. The two requests are connected. The second petition

> 'Through the Spirit, God is already working in history, using human actions to create provisional states of affairs that anticipate the new creation in a real way.'
>
> *Miroslav Volf,*
> Work in the Spirit, *OUP, 1991, p 100*

contains the kingdom in a nutshell, because it links life on earth and life in heaven in the closest possible way.

If we are sincere in praying that God's kingdom should come, then it should have an effect on us. We open ourselves up to being agents of God's will. By simple acts of obedient discipleship, we play a part in bringing the present world into closer conformity with that glorious future age. When situations, structures and individuals *are* changed for the better, we are seeing signs of the kingdom at work.

Helped by the Spirit

Jesus told his followers that if he did not go away, the Spirit could not come, but when he came he would be at work in the world, convicting it of guilt, righteousness and judgment (John 16:7,8). The Holy Spirit is *the* sign of the kingdom, the active presence of God in the world and the guarantee of the kingdom to come (Ephesians 1:13,14). The Spirit was present at creation (Genesis 1:2), and we have seen in an earlier chapter that he inspires our creative, work-related skills. So the gift of the Spirit is part of God's equipment for us to serve him in our workplace, and not just to inspire our 'devotional life'.

Signs of the kingdom

♦ The glow of satisfaction over a beneficial finished product, which has taken a lot of time, money and effort to achieve.

♦ The relief of unravelling manipulative practice, so that confusion and corruption are brushed away, and the true state of affairs is revealed.

♦ The teenager who was a complete pest at school and left with few qualifications, but then knuckles down to get some vocational qualifications and returns to thank the staff for the efforts they made with him.

♦ The breakdown of hierarchical structures which have impeded progress, and the establishment of a new spirit with everybody working towards a common goal.

♦ The cancellation of the backlog of unpayable debts of the poorest countries, to give hope to the impoverished people of the world.

Home work

Throughout this series of studies we have focused mainly on work as paid employment, usually based outside the home. But many people (mostly but not entirely women) work hard as 'home-makers', enabling the chief breadwinner to 'go out to work'. Home-making can be satisfying, but also tiring and frustrating. As we consider the transformation of work in the kingdom of God, we should include the unpaid labour of love offered by such people.

> 'Most women are housewives with prime responsibility for a home and family. More than half of all married women also work outside the home. A quick calculation therefore will indicate that many women have two jobs, often both demanding and full time.'
>
> *Elaine Storkey,* What's Right with Feminism? *SPCK, 1985, p 14*

CHAPTER 5

Practical steps

Having thought and talked our way through a variety of work-related issues, we are still left with the task of having to go to work tomorrow and face those issues! Here are a few more stepping stones to bridge the torrent of pressures:

Draw on God's power Many workers have a strong sense of powerlessness, especially if they occupy junior positions. They may have far-reaching objections to the way the organization is structured, or bemoan the financial constraints under which they are acting. An apt response to that situation may be simply to *confess* your powerlessness, and admit your dependence on God's Spirit.

Find support at work We are not always as powerless as we imagine. If we can find others who think similarly, then it may be possible to voice a different view with some hope of changing things. Such people will not necessarily be fellow-Christians. Some have an excellent grasp of kingdom values without yet having reached the point of acknowledging God as king. There can still be fruitful alliances with them at work. Indeed, co-operation with them on a common project may be a good way of getting to know them better, in turn opening the door to speaking to them explicitly about Christ.

Meet with Christians at work It is valuable to enjoy fellowship with other Christians in our organizations. There are pressure-points which only a fellow-Christian will understand, and sharing a problem can help towards solving it. Many Christians are more isolated in the workplace than they need to be. If it is widely known that you are one, that may encourage others to crawl out of the woodwork.

Make use of wider resources There are organizations and publications which provide useful resources for Christians at work. Page 40 provides a starting-point.

Enlist the support of your church This is where we began in chapter one. Get the church thinking about and praying for the work-related issues which various members face. You may find experience and ideas come from others you had not thought of asking.

Pray together A group of people specially committed to witness in the workplace could meet regularly – perhaps over breakfast before work. Commit each individual's working situation to the Lord. Ask that God will show that person more of his plan for them, their organization or their working sector. Pray that God's Spirit will equip them richly for their work and that he will encourage them through their difficulties.

Aim

To put our daily work into the eternal perspective of God's purposes for the whole world.

1. Bible base

a Read the parable in Luke 19:11-27. Instead of *money,* think of *opportunity* (which is what money represents). Make a list of the opportunities and responsibilities you have for serving God and building his kingdom in your place of work. What are the same opportunities, and what are different ones which group members face?

b Read Isaiah 65:17-25 and Revelation 21:1-8,22-27. What inspiration and encouragement can you glean for your life in the world and the workplace now from these visions of the future?

2. Kingdom people?

Discuss how might 'God's will be done, in my workplace as it is in heaven'. What would count as signs of the kingdom breaking into the current way of doing things? (You could give each group member time to write down a couple of sentences, and then to share them with the group.)

3. What will you do now?

Ask each member of the group to think about the following questions, then to share their thoughts with the rest of the group:

1. Has the attitude I have to my work changed as a result of these sessions? To what extent do I see my work as part of a God-given ministry?

2. What features of the work I am involved in do I believe God wants to change? What practical steps can I take to contribute to that change?

3. How might God be wishing to use me at work during the next few weeks? How can I become a more effective channel for him to use in personal witness and in my contribution to the workplace?

4. How may we encourage our church to put people's working lives higher up its agenda? How might it provide more encouragement and support to people at work?

Useful Resources

Organizations and Contact People

CARE (Christian Action Research and Education) is concerned with education, family, and sanctity of life issues. Rev Lyndon Bowring, CARE, 53 Romney Street, London SW1P 3RF.

CHRISTIANS AT WORK offers advice and encouragement for Christian fellowships in the workplace. Mr Rod Badams, 148 Railway Terrace, Rugby, Warwickshire CV21 3HN.

CHRISTIAN IMPACT relates biblical faith to every aspect of life, and collaborates with the UCCF Business Studies Group. Rev Simon Steer, St Peter's, Vere Street, London W1M 9HP.

CHRISTIANS IN PUBLIC LIFE PROGRAMME helps all Christians involved in public life through conferences and research papers. Dr David Clark, CIPL, Westhill College, Selly Oak, Birmingham B29 6LL.

INDUSTRIAL MISSION ASSOCIATION is a network of industrial chaplains who visit the workplace. Rev Robin Blount, Rivendell, School Lane, Folkestone, Kent CT18 8AY.

INSTITUTE OF BUSINESS ETHICS offers advice to companies wishing to implement effective ethical policies. Mr Stanley Kiaer, 12 Palace Street, London SW1E 5JA.

JUBILEE CENTRE provides a biblical response to key current issues. An offshoot, the Relationships Foundation, promotes quality relationships in public and private life. Dr Michael Schluter, 3 Hooper Street, Cambridge CB1 2NZ.

RIDLEY HALL FOUNDATION runs a programme of seminars relating Christian faith to the business world. Dr Richard Higginson, Ridley Hall, Cambridge CB3 9HG.

UK ACTION is an initiative resourcing evangelical churches addressing issues of inner-city poverty and unemployment. Mr David Evans, Tear Fund, 100 Church Road, Teddington, Middx TW11 8QE.

There are also specific occupational groups, like the Christian Lawyers' Fellowship or the Christian Medical Fellowship.

Books

Graham Dow, *A Christian Understanding of Daily Work,* Grove Pastoral No.57, 1994
Stephen Green, *Serving God? Serving Mammon?* Marshall Pickering, 1996
Mark Greene, *Thank God It's Monday,* Scripture Union, 1994
Richard Higginson, *Called to Account: Adding Value in God's World,* Eagle, 1993; *Transforming Leadership: A Christian Approach to Management,* SPCK, 1996.
Leland Ryken, *Work and Leisure in Christian Perspective,* IVP, 1987
Andrew Stokes, *Working with God,* Mowbray, 1992
Steve Walton, *A Call to Live,* Triangle, 1994
David Westcott, *Work Well: Live Well,* Marshall Pickering, 1996

Magazines and Journals

Ethos is a Christian business magazine. ETHOS Communications Ltd, 15a High Street, Harpenden, Herts AL5 2RT.
Faith in Business is a quarterly journal relating Christian faith to the business world. Dr Ian Groves, 4 Broughton Road, Ipswich, Suffolk IP1 3QR.
Third Way surveys the modern world through Christian eyes. Mr Brian Draper, St Peter's, Sumner Road, Harrow, Middlesex HA2 4BX.